PSALMS OF HOPE

ENCOURAGEMENT THROUGH POETRY

Hope D. Scott

Diligence Publishing Company
Bloomfield, New Jersey

PSALMS OF HOPE: ENCOURAGMENT THROUGH POETRY

To contact the author to speak at your church, organization, seminar or conference email:
hopespsalms@gmail.com

PSALMS OF HOPE: ENCOURAGMENT THROUGH POETRY

ISBN 978-1-7331353-8-2

Printed in the United States

TABLE OF CONTENTS

INTRODUCTION

The words "Psalms of Hope" came to me years ago. It's actually a play on words. Yes, Hope is my name but mainly the "Hope" in the title is to GIVE HOPE to others. I am a firm believer in encouragement. Many people, especially during these times, feel invisible. They feel alone. They need hope. I've felt that way and know what it is to have someone give you a warm smile, a kind word or even an unexpected gift. It was something about that one-on-one contact that made me feel SEEN and valued. The Bible has so much to say about encouragement. It is SO important. An encouraging word can change a mind, mood, and even a life decision. It can literally silence the voice of the enemy in a person's mind. Your words of encouragement to someone could be that pivotal point in their lives that they will always remember.

"Psalms of Hope" is written for you and for whomever you come in contact with. One of these poems could come to mind to share with someone. They were written in prayer. They were written out of experience. They were designed to speak directly to the heart of some situations. I pray that you are encouraged.

Hope D. Scott

PURPOSE DEFINED

Fearfully and wonderfully made,
Beautifully, so
Created for purpose
Your own, unique flow.

That thing that ignites your passion
And has your heart and The Father's entwined
Giving Him Glory through your praise and talents
It's your purpose, defined.

Things will come to distract you
Life, circumstances
Sometimes, we try to do it all
But, prayer and praise, you must not ignore
Because it is the Master's call.

Do not despise small beginnings
Keep pressing on; His favor you'll find
Don't let it go, don't lay it down or never pick it up because
of your daily grind.

The place of worship and moving in destiny
Is the place we need to be
The place where peace and provision reside
And God gets all the Glory.

Don't fret if you don't have the full picture
Your main purpose is to praise
Continue to stay in connection with Him
And prepare to be amazed!

PERFECT IMPERFECT ME

Perfect Imperfect Me
Formed sight unseen
But purposed to be
Perfectly formed imperfect me

Perfectly made in His image
But imperfect, I carry some flaws
Excuse me while I learn to be patient with ME
And allow Him to knock down some walls

Fearfully and wonderfully made
I am called and have in me the ability
To be perfect
As I cooperate in this dance of imperfect perfection
I'm being refined – defined
By The Perfect One
Imperfect? Yes, but still connected to the vine

Perfect Him dwells in imperfect me
My yielding to Him determines
How much of Him you'll see
Imperfection can't lean on its own ability
But lean on The Perfect One
In perfect Humility

Dancing together, we are in sync
By this, perfection outweighs imperfection
Even though a little imperfection might remain
Perfection makes sure it doesn't take a prideful gain

Each new day is a blessing
A new mercy has begun
An opportunity to give my imperfections to Perfection
Knowing the battle is already won

Loving Perfection because even though my imperfection He sees
He still loves Perfect Imperfect Me

TROUBLES OF THE CALLING

Got the Heavenly Call and said "Yes"
Joy Full, Lives are changed
No greater feeling in the world than walking just
As created and designed.

New crowd of people, new demands
More pulling, more fans
More fame, more plans
Life is looking grand.

Influences come to pull away
You've decided you will not stray
But, you look up one day
And the "joy" of the call is gone
Everybody else's desires for you have won.

Reality check, self-evaluate, repentance, regenerate.
Putting God back on the throne
Leaving all the "extras" alone
Giving Him back His seat as first
Saying "no" to others' thirst.

Simplicity, reorganization.
Remaining True.
That can be hard to do.
When everyone is pulling you.
If God is first and that remains,

He'll help you in the juggling game.
In such a way that many call on His name
And you won't have to live up to the "fame."

"Burnout" will not be the norm for you.
Because He'll see you through.
Periods of rest He'll arrange for you....

HE

Nothing to fear
No need to worry
We are children
And our Daddy is God!

He dries all our tears
He gives us joy and peace
He showers us with love
He renews us in Him!

He shows us Himself
He is the Lord
His handiwork is undeniable
He is God!

When we need a Savior
He'll save our soul
When we need a healer
He'll make us whole.

When we need a breakthrough
He'll give us strength to push
When we need a reminder
Remember the burning bush-

"I AM THE AM," He says, always present
No matter what the issue
When we cry
He'll send His comfort
As tissue

He is the "I AM"
He is The One
He is above ALL
Our Everything

He keeps us enclosed in walls of protection
Surrounds us with Angels of flame
We are covered and loved
Praise His Name!

TAKE YOUR PLACE

I don't want to be my own God
In my life, I don't want the throne
I decrease and give you full authority
I don't want to do this life on my own

I say that you are "Lord"
But in some things, I maintain control
I want to build and manage my walls
Instead of releasing my hold

I repent of that
I surrender my life's reigns
From going my own way, I refrain

My life is not my own
You are my Lord, I'm not my own
Take your place, take your seat
In my heart, my soul, my life
Take your place on the throne

IN THE MEANTIME

There is a place of "in-between"
"Not where we want to be" but "not where we used to be"
This can be an uncomfortable place!

Ready to go on with what we need to get on with
Ready to fulfill destiny
Ready to find our place
But, knowing that we still have much to learn.

The Lord will not take us too fast but,
At the pace where it does the most good.
Not pleasing to us, but
He knows our end.
He knows what's best for us.

So I pray and praise and trust
All along knowing that Christ will perfect that which
Concerns me
Trying not to lean on my own understanding
Praying that I learn all that He wants to teach me
Knowing my timing is not His.
He has me right where He wants me.
So, instead of being impatient or frustrated,
In the meantime, I'll learn more of Him

Praise Him more
Thank Him more
Worship Him more
And
Learn to wait on Him.

THE SOUND

LISTEN:
Can you hear that sound?
It's a drumbeat that is beginning
To get louder in the hearts of man.

Right now, it is ever so light
A beating and a vibrating sound
Only the most sensitive can hear it now.

But, as it begins to get louder (and it will)
It will shake the hearts of the troops
And they will begin to come together in formation
Where the One True God is Lord.

Our Holy Armor is firmly strapped in place
Ready to do battle for The Lord
We will be at attention and equipped
And girded with the sword.

Signs and wonders will once again fill the earth
No one will be able to deny
The one who sits on the throne
The one who sits on high!

Again, do you hear it?

The sound. A drumbeat in your spirit.

Get quiet. Seek Him. Get into position.
Allow yourself to be trained.
You'll begin to hear it, but do not fear it.

It's the sound of a calling, a gathering cry
Sent out from The Lord.
Get into position – be ready.
What's at hand?
The Lord.

SEASONS

Longest winter, frigid waters
Trees living- but season of barrenness has overtaken
Forward movement gone into hibernation
So are some seasons of life, when we feel forsaken

Just as a blizzard blows through in its fury
But you're tucked safely inside with a fire burning
So, also let that be the way of your spirit
Taking refuge under the safety of God's wings
Resting in His Son while earthly sun and warmth you're yearning

Hunker down and make use of time
Building your faith while moving and seeking intentionally
While the season is steadily passing
When the new chapter begins and the shift complete
They'll be new wonders, new joy and spiritual strength everlasting

Keep going, keep seeking, keep believing, stand fast
HE is the God of all weather, all seasons
Even when it seems all the seasons are running simultaneously
And you can't figure rhyme nor reason

He is the Anchor. He is the Steady
The Common Denominator. The Regulator
Even when the seasons rage
Let Him take center stage
And orchestrate your New Beginning

YOU

One of the biggest mistakes in life is not knowing
Who you are and not realizing your worth.
Having the revelation that there is a reason
for your birth –
Why you dwell on this earth.

You are valued.

You're meant to be here
Your presence on earth required
It doesn't matter the circumstances
Around your birth and other things in life
that might have transpired.

You have a purpose.

You're further than you see yourself
You're better than you think you are
While you're downgrading your life
God thinks you're a star

You are important.

He loves you, He cares
You're in the palm of His hand
See yourself there always
And if you fall, make HIS hand the place you land

You are safe with Him.

The Maker of this world
The Creator of all things
The Ruler of Heaven and Earth
Yet over YOU He rejoices and sings

You are His Masterpiece.

I DANCE WITH MY FATHER

I dance.
We dance. We twirl.
No greater liberty I feel in this world
Chivalry is never dead with you
In your arms I can glide
No hidden places in you
Matter of fact, I don't want to hide

With outstretched arms I run to you
Your wings are my refuge
To them, I make haste
You cover me with Your feathers
You cover me with Your Grace

With a broad smile I bow
I raise my arms and eyes in wonder
To look upon my Savior's face
Whose eyes shine like the sun
Not from Him but to Him, I run

With sweet abandon and overwhelming joy
I twirl in His presence and know He is pleased
Proud of me in my imperfect uniqueness
His Creation. His Seed.

You lead me by still waters
I rest in peace on soft, green grass
I'm safe with you
Your faithfulness and love hold fast

I dance before and with My Father
We're one. He in I and I in Him
Joy and Peace is complete
As I dance before and with My Father

STRATEGY OF LOVE

If Prayer of Love is chosen – and its actions – it travels
Love can go to places we can't
Love can go to places we won't
Love can go to places we don't

This is true. I've seen it.
Love in action, love in motion.
Where there is chaos, this strategy weaves through the commotion
And hits the heart that least expects it
And the hearts in which it was sent
And, ALSO changes/covers/blesses the heart of the person from whom
The prayer was sent.

Love covers, Love Shifts, Love changes
Love rearranges

Makes them throw down the stone before their hands can eject it
It can cast down lies that have been erected
Change a course – make a person correct it.

There is also peace
Sweet release – from grief
For those that choose to receive
Love can achieve
What we in our flesh won't believe

It's a mystery, an effective strategy
That some will think is foolish
But done in sincerity and obedience
It will yield rewards to those that do this.

WHAT I IMAGINE HE'S SAYING

If you could see what I see
And know what I know
You'd not have a single doubt
Of the goodness I show

Ever with you, I have never
Left your side
I put my Spirit in you
To be your guide

I know right now a better place is hard to imagine
It seems you've been where you are for so long
But, remember times and seasons are changing
I'm with you and giving you a new song

New wine you've prayed for
New wine you'll surely be given
For the old wineskin has been peeled away
And oppression – far from you – has been driven

So, place your faith in me
Don't doubt my leading in your next steps
Don't believe all you see
What I've told you, it's so. I am your help

Know that all I've said is true
I'll truly ALWAYS be with you
Get ready to smile with joy unspeakable, down in your soul

Let love and trust be your goal – As your destiny, before
you, I unfold.

YOUR EXPRESSION

We were created to glorify
We were created to praise
Each given his/her own unique expression(s)
A personal, fulfilling way

Your sound is different from any others
It's needed to make the song complete.
God listens for your specific melody
Don't allow any fear, distractions to make your sound retreat

It might not be a common talent,
Your expression unto God might be different.
Not readily received or valued by religious sisters and brothers
But, as long as He leads you and it's done unto Him
His opinion matters above all others.

Don't think your talent is small or insignificant
It's given to glorify God but, also to make YOUR heart sing.
Your expression makes a joyful noise and blesses the earth
But, also releases a sound that makes Heaven ring!

Know you are uniquely made and gifted
No one is like you or can duplicate your sound
Use your talents, stir up the gift
And make your Heavenly Father Proud!

BEFORE AND AFTER

Days are busy, filled with noise
Sometimes chaotic, quietness destroyed.
Thoughts run like freight trains
Meeting here, gotta go there
Hamsters on a wheel
Going nowhere.

He calls me to a place
A place of being still.
I silence my heart, cease my thoughts before Him
Focus on Him and His Will.

Knowing that to do this is worship unto Him
Because I've ceased my busy to spend time with Him.
He refreshes and restores. We love on each other.
I'm thankful. I praise. He is like no other.

Now, I'm ready to go out again
Refreshed and renewed
I'm not so wound up in my busy
That to Him I can't be used.
I'm available, not bound
I'm not so tightly wound
His Light and Joy is able to shine though me
So others can see His Glory
And be drawn to His life-changing Story

AWE

My eyes look and behold your beauty...
My eyes see it but there's simply
   not enough "looking" I can do to take it all in.
My two eyes try to absorb it all at once
But they, nor my brain
   can comprehend the magnitude of
Your Majesty.
The entire totality of your Glory.

My flesh cannot find words
That my spirit wants to express!

If I run-that's not enough.
If I scream and shout-that's not enough.
If I had 10,000 tongues, that's not enough
To express all that I behold.

He gives me just enough-right beneath
   all I can take
Because if I beheld Him anymore than now,
I would simply be no more.
I would simply be gone.
But, it's not time yet. There's a lot of work still to be done.
So, I decide to stay in awe of you, no matter what
Cause you are bigger and better than anyone or anything
   I've ever known
Let my awe of you keep me before your throne.

THEY WEREN'T READY!

Religion wasn't ready for your gift so they turned it aside
Instead of inviting your Godly expression-they didn't understand
So, they gave it rejection
Which instituted your near defection
Before you really got a chance to know who Jesus Is.

Religion doesn't seem to understand - that it's God that gifts man
With whatever expression of praise He chooses
Whatever method HE uses
To get HIS Glory on earth–
I might not sing like a bird, but I can rhyme unto The Lord
And HE sees that worth

Even if Religion don't
Even if Religion refuses to or won't
Even if Religion judges what I do
And say it's not the Christian way

He sees my REALNESS – my expression to Him in the gift He gave.
I give Him Glory because He forgave – saved me from a fiery grave.
So, in front of Religion – I might not behave
How your religious minds might see
But... hey... I'm free? Are you?
What expression has He called you to?

Not one that judges, hold grudges or have a resting face in hate.
He's called us by His Grace
The gift Glorifies Him and gives us the joy
To run this race

So, don't hold it down just cause it might not fit – what religion looks
Like today.
That expression is inside trying to manifest outside – don't let its
Unpopularity keep it hidden.
This expression has been bidden – Allow it to come forth.

THE COLOR OF MY SKIN

The Color of my skin does not define me
But what I carry in my heart
The Words that come out of my mouth
And the way that I treat you,
Should tell you a lot.

The color of my skin does not tell you
The next thing I'll say or do.
The problem with a stereotype is,
It gives a distorted point of view,
We don't give people a chance
We look at the color of their skin
And dismiss without another glance

The color of my skin does not make me more beautiful,
Although, beautiful I am
Because I am made in the image of My Heavenly Father
The One and Only Great I Am

The Color of my skin does not determine my ability to be great
For greatness lies within each one of us
It's the evil that LIES that makes skin color such a fuss.
The Father made skin colors different to continue to show His Majesty
And His Creative beauty
In and on our images.
So, we would look at each other and see beauty and not judgment
And fulfill all His purposes

No, the color of my skin does not define me
For we all have the power to make or break each other–
And ourselves as well.
My skin color will not determine whether I go to Heaven or Hell.

My skin color reminds me that before I was born, I was molded in the
Master's Hands.

I did not choose my color, He did and I will walk proud displaying His Wonderful handiwork.
Whether I'm Black or White, Red or Brown
I am His masterpiece.
I will remember that man's standards will never be God's
I'm always special in HIS EYES.
The color of my skin, He'll never mock or despise.
For I am His prize.

Remember all who've gone before you
The Leaders, The Activists, The Inventors
The History Changers, The History Makers
In spite of adversity, Greatness won
I will put myself in that category and rise up to be the next one
Because it's not too late
No, my skin color does not define me, nor will it stop me from being GREAT!

ENCOURAGEMENT

You will not be an unfinished story
What He promised, He will do
He has not forgotten
The promises He made to you

He is the Author and the Finisher
The work He started in you will be completed
He will get the glory out of your story
Do not allow your faith to be depleted

Don't be distracted by what your eyes see
Stand on His Word and what He has spoken,
Decree!

Believe! Stay in Faith!
Stay connected! Do not waver!
For in due time, His promises will come to pass
And you'll be showered with His favor!

BREATHE

Breath is precious
A gift. A grace
I inhale you in
I breathe you out
YOU are my breath.

I forget everything going on around me
I sit with you
And, just breathe

I reflect on my blessings
How you've bought me through trials
When you never left me,
Was right beside me
During the times I felt exiled

I breathe slower and relax
As I rest in the memories of victories past

I breathe in relief reminding myself
That this situation might be different
But, you are the same God
That never changes

Thank you for that assurance
Thank you for breathing life into me
Thank you for the ability to breathe
Thank you for regulating that breathing as I put my
Trust in you

DOING THE FIRST THING LAST

Coming boldly to Your Throne
Humbly, I bow
I now know that you're in control
And I need you now

I tried to fix it all myself
And made more of a mess
I feel so helpless and confused
And ask you to give me rest

Forgive me that I tried all these things
Instead of coming to you first
Thank you for your Grace and Mercy
That stepped in before things got worse

I lay my troubles at your feet
No longer trusting in my own strength
Please council me on this and I will follow your lead
Knowing in you, I will succeed.

Remind me when I try to do it all on my own
That you're with me, I'm never alone
May I then correct my course and seek your wisdom first.

YOUR PURPOSE OVER MY PLANS

I don't know how I got here
This life is not what I planned
But, through all my trials and disappointments
I am still in your hands

Every day is not perfect
I have my smiles and my frowns
But Lord, you are my steady constant
Your faithfulness never lets me down

I am learning how to trust and praise
And lean not unto my own understanding
When I rest in you and trust the process,
Living this life seems less demanding

I've learned there are no mistakes in you
And no matter how my life is, I love you
So, it'll work out for my good
My life will give you Glory
And as I trust you, it'll work
Out as it should

I thank you for ordering my steps
Because you can see what I don't
I'm safe with you. I surrender my plans
I lay them down and humbly, take your hand

THERE

I come to you
Ready to lament and collapse
With crying

Instead, you shower me
With your love, joy and laughter
My tears, you end up drying!

I laugh and laugh
As you envelope me with your love and care
I would do anything to just stay
THERE

THERE where time ceases to exist
And there's just me and you
Issues just fade away
And I become unglued

I dance, I sing, I praise
Your Glory I raise
THERE in THAT place where you are found
My troubles cease, my mind becomes sound
And, as I dwell, peace abounds

FLINTY FACE

The trivial things of this life
Its cares, its worries cannot overly matter
When I entangle myself in them
My focus is lost and begins to scatter

I regroup and, in faith
I speak to those things
That try to distract me and get me off course
And confusion bring

I refuse to be entangled
With debates of unprofitable chatter
When God has chosen me to be His soldier
And I must stay focused on the battle

I'm on the wall, my assignment given
I will please Him who has called me
Like a flint I am set and will not be put to shame
I will bring Glory to His Name!

TAKING MY REFUGE

Lord, there is not one area
In my life
That doesn't need a touch from you
All areas require your grace and attention
I need you so much and in so many situations
Some things, I can talk over with friends
But other things,
ONLY to you I can mention

Issues and problems seem to come consistently
But I know you can deliver my soul in peace
From every battle coming up against me

When my knees begin to buckle
Under the weight of the test
You cover me with songs of deliverance
They surround me to relieve the stress

I lay before you my heart and all that's inside
You bring deliverance with your peace and Your Word
And tell me, in YOU to hide
You delivered me when I cried
In your Word, I choose to abide

There is no safety apart from you
Your Presence I must feel
In every nook and cranny of my life
I'm opening my heart to place your seed

I give permission for your throne
To be set up in my soul, my mind, my heart
I submit and let you do your work
Making sure I do my part

I'm available, I'm making space for you to come in
Lord, I need you
Revive me, again

CLOUDS OR FOG

I would rather soar in the clouds
Than be surrounded by fog

Jumping in and out of clouds
Joyful and free
Or blinded by the fog and not able to see what
Is right in front of me

Clouds do carry a risk but,
I can rise above the thunder
While if I choose the fog,
I can't see and chances are, I'll blunder

I'd rather tune in to THE VOICE
The one that dwells beyond the clouds
Than listen to the many voices that linger in the fog
Screaming ignorantly and loud

In fog, stumbling, blinded by opinions
Surrounded by the noise
Judgment smoky and full of disdain
In the fog, living life void
OR
Riding HIGH among the clouds
Seeking Heavenly wisdom – being shown a greater view
Walking in the Love, Peace and Joy
That some in the fog had once dwelled or never knew

And if in the fog, it's not too late to rise,
Come to Him, He'll clear the fog so you can see the sky
And begin to live out loud, among the clouds
To see from a higher point of view

MY BELOVED

Out of the wilderness I come, leaning on my beloved
He wasn't my beloved when I went in, but He is now
And, I won't let Him go

He has stood by His Word and never lied
He has always provided and never left my side
He's always counseled me and been my guide
From Him, I CAN NOT, I CHOOSE NOT to hide
In Him, I abide

Through the wilderness, He has kept my mind
When it threatened to shatter
Through the hurt and everything concerning me,
He let me know that TO HIM, I MATTER

As insignificant as some things can be
It mattered to Him because it mattered to me
Because of my beloved, I now can see

Yes, I can lean boldly and without shame on my
Beloved,
Jesus is His name
He walked through the wilderness first
So, then He could walk through it with me
I'm walking out of this wilderness with my Beloved,
totally free!

FEAR

Fear is a shadow
Lurking in hiding
Trying to dismount
Where you are abiding

Press on in spite of
Let faith conquer fear
You are with me, stay with me
I'm always near

Don't succumb to the shadows
Trying to speak different rules to the game
Remember my Word and my promises
Focus on my name

You resist him, he'll flee
In you, he'll find no place
Speak my word, move forward
Continue the race
   -God

REST

I didn't call you to walk the floor in worry
I've called you to rest in my arms
Go back to bed and enjoy sweet sleep
And be released from all alarm

Abide and take your rest in me
I have it all in control
Your job is to praise and have faith in me
Through it all, ONTO ME, HOLD

I'll provide, I'll supply
On me, rely
I'm your Father, I take care of what's mine
No matter who your earthly father is,
I AM GOD. I AM DIVINE

Take all that worry
And all that fear
Everything that you hold dear and
Lay it at my feet

And rest dear child
Get sweet sleep in me
Release control and let me take my seat

I got this. I got you
Let me handle these things while you
Rest in me
And be released.

IT IS WELL WITH MY SOUL

When chaos is all around me
My heart is at ease
The Lord says He'll protect me
It is well with my soul

Though tempest rise and fall
And we don't know when the next waves will collide
It is well with my soul
In Him, I'll abide

He is the ultimate authority
He sits enthroned above the circle of the earth
Come what may, it is will with my soul
I'll trust in the one who gives me worth

I have given Him His Kingship over my life
I live It through Him, consistency is my goal
He knows the end from the beginning and is watching over it all
So, I'll keep it well with my soul.

JOYOUS PRAISE!

Hallelujah!
Praise the Lord in everything
Hallelujah!
Glory to God! He reigns!

Hallelujah!
We give you Joyful Praise
We come to you again

To tell you how marvelous you are
And give you Glory and praise
It all belongs to you!
Our worship we raise

We dance and shout before you
We send you our love
We glorify you on the inside of our hearts and we
Shout and send love above

Your Glory will be seen
And all the earth will know
That you are The King of Glory
Your power you are about to show

All eyes will behold you!
All knees will bow to your open splendor
All tongues will confess that you are Lord
And your Glory we will render

Hallelujah!
Holy, Holy, Holy
All Glory belongs to you and you alone
Hallelujah to the Almighty one
That sits on the throne!

AMEN!

ABOUT THE AUTHOR

Hope D. Scott, also known as "The Limitless Lady," is a graduate of Elizabeth City State University and a Certified Life Coach. She is an accomplished writer, poet, and performer of Spoken Word through the art of dance. She is the mother of two phenomenal daughters, Uneque and Charity. Hope most recently launched her blogsite "Hopepsalms.com."

It has always been her passion to support, encourage and inspire others through writing, spoken word and poetry. Hope's passion was evidenced as she penned her first poem when she was five (5) years of age. She is the author of *"To Encourage You: Poems, Inspirational Writings and Affirmations."* Hope was also privileged to serve as co-author of *"A Reason To Be."* A favorite quote found on her blog site is "Don't be fooled by the fragile and peaceful presentation of a butterfly. It had to go through a life-threatening process so it could show its beauty."

Life's process has caused the beauty of encouragement and inspiration to be released in Hope's writings.

ORDER INFORMATION

You can order additional copies of *Psalms of Hope: Encouragement Through Poetry* by emailing the author directly using the email address below.

Hope D. Scott

Email Address:

hopespsalms@gmail.com

Books are available at Amazon.com, BN.com Kindle and Your Local Bookstores (By Request)

.

Please leave a review for this book on Amazon and let other readers know how much you enjoyed reading it.

Thank you!